CONTENTS

HIGH-POWERED WORDS 4

GET ON THE WAVELENGTH 6

Wonderful H₂O 8

Erosion and Weathering 10

When Wonderful Turns Wicked 12

   Drought 12

   A Thirsty World 14

   Floods 16

   Out of Control 18

Taming the Rivers 20

Traveling on Water 22

Watering the Land 24

The Blue Revolution 26

Conserving Wetlands 28

AFTERSHOCKS 30

GLOSSARY 32

INDEX 32

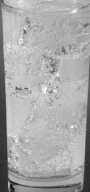

conservation the protection of the environment, plants, and animals

debris (*duh BREE*) the remains of something broken down; litter

evaporate (*e VAP uh rate*) to change from a liquid into a gas, or vapor

irrigation (*ear uh GAY shun*) the supply of water to farmland, usually by human-made methods

lagoon (*luh GOON*) an area of shallow water that is connected to a sea or an ocean

organism (*OR guh niz uhm*) a living thing

For easy reference, see Wordmark on back flap.
For additional vocabulary, see Glossary on page 32.

The word *debris* is a French word that is now part of the English language. Some common synonyms for the word *debris* are: *rubble*, *trash*, *rubbish*, and *junk*.

Venice, Italy, is built on a **lagoon**. The water levels in the lagoon change. This causes frequent, serious flooding in the city.

Water is the earth's most precious **resource**. It can be both wicked and wonderful. People have found ways to use water for power and to grow crops. We can travel over water. We can enjoy water sports. Water also causes some of the worst problems around the world, such as flooding and erosion.

Water is essential to life. Only 2.5 percent of all water on the earth is freshwater. Today, the earth's population is about six billion. By 2050, the population is expected to be about nine billion. However, the amount of fresh, clean water is not increasing.

In many parts of the world, people wait anxiously for rain. Some places get a great deal. Some get little. Scientists and engineers around the world are working out ways to bring water to dry places. They also try to control water in places that have too much of it.

OUR WATERY WORLD

Water is everywhere on the earth. However, only 2.5 percent of it is freshwater.

Oceans and other salt water

Oceans cover 71 percent of the earth. They contain 96.5 percent of all the water on the earth.

Ice and snow

Nearly 70 percent of the earth's freshwater is frozen in **glaciers**, snow, and ice.

Groundwater

Thirty percent of all freshwater is under the ground. Most of it is hard to reach.

Lakes and rivers

Lakes and rivers contain just a little more than 0.25 percent of all freshwater.

Soils and wetlands

These contain just under 0.1 percent of all freshwater.

Atmospheric

Clouds and water **vapor** hold just 0.04 percent of all freshwater.

WONDERFUL H₂O

All **organisms** need water. The human body is made up mostly of water. We take in water from food and drink. We take in moisture in the air we breathe. The scientific name for water is hydrogen oxide. In 1805, two scientists named Joseph Louis Gay-Lussac and Alexander von Humboldt studied water **molecules** closely. They discovered that water contains two volumes of hydrogen (H) for every one volume of oxygen (O). That's why the chemical symbol for water is H_2O.

Water molecule

Joseph Louis Gay-Lussac

Alexander von Humboldt

Water is a wonderful substance. It is the only substance that can exist in three states at ordinary temperatures. These states are solid, liquid, and gas. Changes between these states are necessary to life on the earth. For example, the change from a gas to a liquid is an important part of the water cycle.

Water has many forms. It can be ice and snow. It can be water vapor, fog, or simply liquid water.

Water Facts

- exists in three states at normal temperatures
- H_2O is its chemical symbol
- makes up most of human body
- scientific name is hydrogen oxide

THE WATER CYCLE

The same water that fell as rain millions of years ago is still falling on the earth today. The water in oceans and lakes **evaporates**. It becomes water vapor. High in the sky, this **condenses** into tiny droplets and forms clouds. The water held in clouds falls back to earth as rain, hail, sleet, or snow. This process is called the water cycle.

4. Water falls back to earth as rain, hail, sleet, or snow.

3. Water vapor condenses into clouds.

2. Some water evaporates and becomes water vapor.

5. Rain flows into rivers. It soaks into underground pools and streams.

1. Oceans and lakes absorb heat from the sun.

6. Rivers and underground streams return water to oceans and lakes.

EROSION AND WEATHERING

The earth's landscape is constantly changing. Have you ever watched a pile of mud when it rains? Some of it washes away. Channels and ruts are left. Water and weather shape the earth's **crust** in the same way. The processes that cause this are weathering and erosion. They slowly break down even the hardest rock.

Grand Canyon

THE MAKING OF A GIANT GORGE

Millions of years ago, an area of land in Colorado was forced upward by the movement of the earth's crust. The land rose up to make hills and high areas of rock. Since that time, the Colorado River has been carving its way through the rock. Weathering and erosion caused by the river itself have created a huge **gorge**. The gorge is called the Grand Canyon.

At first, I wasn't sure what the word *landscape* meant. As I read on, it became clear that it meant all the land on the earth. Reading on or rereading often helps me figure out new words.

WHAT'S THE DIFFERENCE?

Weathering: This is the slow breaking down of rocks. Heat, wind, and cold dry out rocks. This causes them to split and crumble. Rocks are also eaten away by chemicals in rainwater. They can even be broken up by plant roots.

Erosion: This is the breaking down and carrying away of rock. Glaciers, streams, oceans, and wind can pick up and carry away rock fragments. These small pieces of rock scrape and carve the surface of other rocks. This breaks them down.

WHEN WONDERFUL TURNS WICKED

DROUGHT

There are many problems facing the world today. The shortage of freshwater is one of the most serious. Water is essential for life. A shortage of clean freshwater in some countries puts thousands of lives at risk. Extreme dryness, or drought, can bring about fire, famine, destruction, and death. Drought occurs when there is not enough water for a long time.

In Africa, many people depend on **agriculture** for their survival. Lack of water causes crops and animals to die. This can lead to a shortage of food. If drought lasts, it can result in famine. Africa has had many terrible droughts and famines.

Food is given out to victims of famine in Ethiopia in the 1980s.

There is a subheading under the main heading. I think this means that "Drought" is just the first in a series of "wicked" things featured on the next few pages.

Dry, red soil in the Australian desert

DRIED UP!

Australia is the driest continent inhabited by people. In 2003, a long drought began. It is the worst in a thousand years in Australia. Australia's largest river system is the Murray-Darling. It is almost dry. Big cities in Australia do not have enough water. In these places, water-recycling plans have been put into action. One major city, Perth, has built a **desalination** plant. The plant turns seawater into drinking water.

In extreme drought conditions, wilderness and farmland become very dry. Terrible fires break out. Once these fires start to spread, they are difficult to stop. On December 3, 2006, fires raged through Whiteman Park. This area is near Perth. The fires were out of control. People had to leave the area to stay safe. Luckily, no one was hurt. However, about 4,000 people had to leave their homes.

SHOCKER

In 1980, Uganda in Africa suffered a drought and famine. Twenty-one percent of the population died. Sixty percent of the children died.

A THIRSTY WORLD

About one billion people around the world do not have access to clean water. Many spend much of each day walking to fetch what water they can find. This water might come from a river or lake. The water often contains disease-carrying bacteria. People become **infected** with diseases. These diseases can be life-threatening.

In 2003, China suffered its worst drought for 50 years. Wells and reservoirs dried up. Millions of people and livestock were left thirsty. Drought-relief programs brought tanks of water from places in China that were unaffected. This water was **rationed**.

People lining up for water in China

Billion is an interesting word. The prefix *bi-* usually means "two." However, one billion is not two million, but 1,000 million. A trillion is a million million, not three million.

Women collecting water in Africa

BUILDING WELLS

In some parts of Sudan, Africa, women walk for seven hours in 115-degree heat to fetch drinkable water. Charities have helped to build wells in villages. Wells are expensive to build. They are often difficult to build as they have to go deep underground. Deep wells can tap into groundwater. This water is not affected by the heat. These wells give people easy access to fresh, clean water.

SHOCKER

Each year, more than five million people die from water-borne diseases, such as cholera. Every day, almost 10,000 children in developing countries die from drinking polluted water.

FLOODS

Sometimes water turns wicked. Floods are a water-related disaster. They are very destructive. There are three main kinds of floods: coastal, river, and flash floods.

Coastal floods occur when strong winds whip up high waves. The waves flow over barriers. They flood inland areas. Some of the worst coastal flooding is caused by hurricanes. They can create enormous tides called storm surges. This kind of flooding happens regularly in Bangladesh. This country's land occupies a flat floodplain. It has numerous rivers and streams that also flood the land.

People in Bangladesh struggle through flooded streets.

Thames Barrier

The Thames
Barrier was
built to control
flooding on the
River Thames in London,
England. It was finished in 1984.
The barrier is about 1,720 feet wide.
It is made up of steel gates. They are 34.5 feet high. They weigh
1,650 tons. The floodgates can open or shut. They are usually left
open so that ships can pass. The gates are closed if weather reports
suggest there is a risk of flooding. The river traffic is stopped.
Then the small gates are closed, followed by the main gates,
one at a time. On average, the barrier is closed four times a year.

ANNUAL FLOODING

Not all river floods are bad. In ancient
Egypt, the flooding of the Nile River was
very important. It helped the population
survive. The ancient Egyptians were
able to grow crops around the Nile.
The annual flooding brought **nutrients**
that made the soil good for farming.

17

Flash floods happen quickly. They can be deadly. Flash floods occur after heavy downpours. They can also occur after a sudden release of water, such as when a dam gives way. The water races down valleys and roads, and through cities. As the flow of water is funneled through narrow gaps, it speeds up. Everything in its path is swept away. Destruction and **debris** are left behind.

SHOCKER

America's worst flash flood occurred in May 1889. The South Fork Dam near Johnstown, Pennsylvania, gave way. The wall of water swamped the town. It killed at least 2,200 people.

In 1992, heavy rain in France caused some rivers to flood. Forty-two people in the area were killed. Many homes and businesses were severely damaged. Here, muddy water races through the streets of Vaison-la-Romaine, France.

SLIDING INTO THE SEA

Venice, Italy, is a unique city. It was built hundreds of years ago on islands in a lagoon. Instead of streets, Venice has hundreds of canals. Each year, the lagoon floods the city. The flooding occurs at different times of the year. It is caused by tides and rain. Venice's buildings and squares are under water for many days. The flooding has caused serious damage to the buildings. The whole city is actually sinking slowly into the sea. Time is running out! There are major plans to build floodgates to stop the tides from flooding the city. **Venetians** and tourists alike hope the floodgates will be built in time to save Venice.

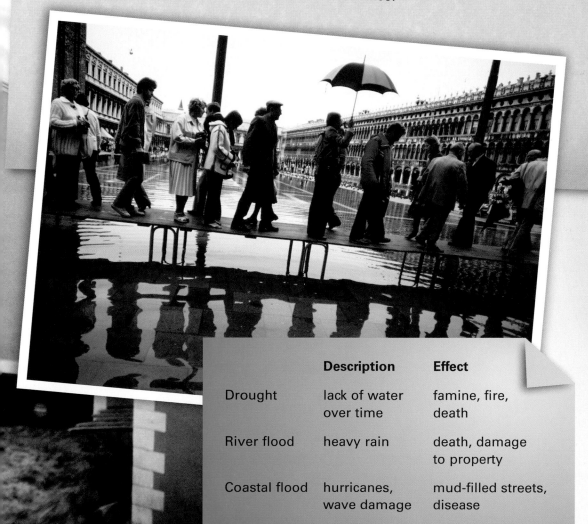

	Description	Effect
Drought	lack of water over time	famine, fire, death
River flood	heavy rain	death, damage to property
Coastal flood	hurricanes, wave damage	mud-filled streets, disease
Flash flood	heavy rain	death, damage to property

TAMING THE RIVERS

Rivers are an important source of water for homes, businesses, and agriculture. Dams are built across rivers to slow the water or redirect it. Dams often create **reservoirs**. These are used to store water. The water can then be channeled or piped to where it is needed. Some dams also harness the energy of the moving water to produce electricity.

Building dams can be **controversial**. The space needed for a reservoir often means that villages, farmland, and forests are flooded. People have to leave their homes. Sometimes historical sites are completely covered by water.

The two temples of Abu Simbel in Egypt had to be moved when a dam was built on the Nile River. The temples were rebuilt exactly as they had been. But they were rebuilt at a spot 200 feet higher than before.

The Three Gorges dam is partly built. The main wall was completed in 2006. The reservoir behind the dam covers a huge area.

THE THREE GORGES DAM

The Yangtze River in Central China is 3,434 miles long. In 1998, more than 2,000 people died when the river flooded. The Chinese government decided to build a dam on the Yangtze. This dam is called the Three Gorges Dam. It will help prevent flooding. It will also produce electricity for the needs of modern China. The dam is one of the largest construction projects in the world.

The dam will be more than 600 feet high. It will be more than a mile wide. However, a reservoir must be created. Any villages that are in the way will be flooded. People living there will have to move away.

SHOCKER

In India, more than 38 million people have been displaced by large-scale dams.

These people in China have had to leave their homes. Their village will be flooded to build the Three Gorges Dam.

TRAVELING ON WATER

Rivers are often used for transportation. However, many rivers have rapids, waterfalls, and other steep sections. Locks and other human-made technology can overcome these obstacles.

To go to a higher or lower level of water, a boat often passes through a lock. The boat enters the lock. Gates close behind it. **Sluices** under water are opened. Water rushes in if the boat is to be raised. If the boat is being lowered, the water in the lock rushes out. The boat rises or falls with the water level. Finally, the water level in the lock is the same as the level of the water the boat is about to enter. The gates ahead open. The boat goes on its way.

The boat is in the lock. Before the water is let into the lock, the boat is still at the lower level.

Lock gate

Boat

Lock gate

CBB TUNNEL

Sometimes water is a barrier. Bridges can be built to span water. Tunnels can go below water. The Chesapeake Bay Bridge and Tunnel (CBBT) is a combination of the two. The CBBT crosses over and under the water. It is the largest bridge-tunnel system in the world. It spans 17.6 miles, coast to coast.

Bridge

Tunnel

Boat

Raised water level

Lock gate

I thought a lock was something to keep people out. So I had some trouble figuring out how locks helped with rivers. Looking carefully at the photographs and captions really helped me understand what this kind of lock does.

The water level inside the lock has been raised. The gates ahead open. The boat exits the lock.

23

WATERING THE LAND

Farming is one of the biggest industries in the world. This is not surprising when you think that there are about six billion people living on the earth, and they all need feeding! Crops need regular water. **Irrigation** is the method that supplies it.

Rain and flooding are natural forms of irrigation. Other forms of irrigation are designed to **supplement** nature. To do this, water is moved from major water sources, such as lakes or rivers. Channels and pipes are used to take the water to reservoirs or **cisterns**. It is stored there until farmers need to use it. Then it is piped to the irrigation systems that water crops and fields.

Drip irrigation

Irrigation channel across farmland

Water for Irrigation
- piped from lakes and rivers
- stored in reservoirs
- piped to individual farms
- used to water crops

KINDS OF IRRIGATION

- **Overhead or sprinkler**: This is popular for crops. The water is piped to sprinklers. These are spread across the fields. The water is sprayed over a large area. However, some of the water evaporates. This wastes water.

- **Center pivot**: This can be used only on flat fields. A machine with a sprinkler attached moves across the fields. This is good for very large areas.

- **Drip or trickle**: This uses 70 percent less water than other methods. The water goes directly to the plant through a pipe. It is dripped out of holes along the pipe. It is popular for vineyards in which each plant needs to be watered carefully.

SHOCKER
Irrigation uses 70 percent of the earth's available usable freshwater.

THE BLUE REVOLUTION

Will our planet have enough water in the future? That depends on how we use this precious resource. Some people pin their hopes on new technologies. One of these is desalination. This removes the salt from salt water so that it becomes freshwater. After all, the oceans hold most of the earth's water.

Desert countries in the Middle East have started to use desalinated water. Desalination is a good option. However, it is very expensive. Scientists believe that water **conservation** is a better answer to the earth's water problems. The solution is to use less and recycle it.

The expression *pin their hopes on* is called a figure of speech. It is a more interesting way of saying *put their trust in*.

A man takes a drink of water at the Doha desalination plant in Kuwait.

HOW YOU CAN SAVE WATER

Some towns and cities now recycle their wastewater. Wastewater can be treated. It can then be used for irrigation.

In some places, governments are encouraging people to install household tanks to catch rainfall. The water can be used to water gardens or flush toilets. Everyone can help by repairing leaky faucets and brushing their teeth with the faucet turned off!

SHOCKER

Today, the average person uses 45 times as much water as was used per person 300 years ago.

CONSERVING WETLANDS

A wetland is an area that is covered by water for some or all of the year. Wetlands are important **ecosystems**. They are home to many plants and animals that are not found elsewhere. Many wetlands are under threat as human demands for water and land grow. **Environmentalists** say that the time has come to give greater protection to wetlands. Otherwise, they will be lost forever.

The Everglades in Florida is a kind of wetland. A huge amount of water has been drawn off to meet human demands. The number of birds and other animals living there has dropped. Restoring the Everglades will take a long time.

Park rangers are educating young people about the Everglades and its ecosystem.

SAVING THE BOG

In Britain, the wetlands are mainly **peat** bogs. In the past, peat was used as a fuel. This put the bogs at risk. Air cannot penetrate far below the surface of peat. This means that ancient objects have been preserved for thousands of years in the bogs. The bogs have been made a conservation priority by the government.

This is a preserved body of a man who died in 350 B.C. He was found in a peat bog in Denmark.

SHOCKER

Bodies thrown into peat bogs have been perfectly preserved. Some have been found to be 2,000 years old. Even the expressions on their faces have been preserved.

Today, in developed countries, we are encouraged to drink more water. It is good for our health. Some experts say that we should drink at least eight glasses a day. This has given birth to an enormous industry of bottled drinking water. But the bottled water comes at a cost. The plastic used in the bottles comes from oil. Oil is another precious resource.

WHAT DO YOU THINK?

Should we stop the production of bottled water?

PRO

I think manufacturers should stop bottling water. The water that comes out of our faucets is checked by health authorities. It is fine to drink. The pollution from producing bottled water causes big problems for the earth.

Producing plastic bottles uses a large amount of energy. It also produces pollution. Transporting the bottles around the world uses more energy. It produces more pollution. Most plastic bottles are not recycled. Instead, they are thrown into the trash. This leads to landfill problems because plastic does not rot away when it is buried.

CON

I think bottled water is a good idea. The money from it could be used to help with the problems of plastic bottles. People should have to pay a tax on bottled water that goes to help build wells in poorer countries. It could also go to the cost of recycling the bottles.

Go to **http://ga.water.usgs. gov/edu** to learn more about water.

agriculture (*AG ruh kul chur*)
farming; growing and raising
crops and animals for food

cistern (*SISS turn*) a tank for
collecting and storing water

condense to change from a gas
to a liquid

controversial (*kon truh VER shul*)
causing much argument
or disagreement

crust the hard, outer layer
of the earth

desalination (*dee sal uh NAY
shun*) the process of changing
salt water into freshwater

ecosystem (*EE koh siss tuhm*)
a community of animals and
plants interacting with their
environment

environmentalist a person who
works to protect the environment

glacier a large mass of
slow-moving ice

gorge (*GORJ*) a deep valley
with steep, rocky sides

infect to contaminate with
a disease

molecule (*MOL uh kyool*) the
smallest particles into which a
substance can be divided while
staying the same substance

nutrients (*NOO tree uhnts*)
substances that help living things
be healthy and grow

peat marshy soil that is made up
of decomposed plants

ration to allow people to have
items only in limited amounts

reservoir (*REZ ur vor*) a lake
that is used to store water

resource a stock or supply
of materials or assets

sluice a human-made passage
for water, which is used
to control the water's flow

supplement an addition
or support

vapor the gaseous form of
something that is usually liquid

Venetian a person who lives
in the city of Venice, Italy

INDEX

bushfires	13
dams	18, 20–21
diseases	14–15, 19
droughts	12–14, 19
electricity	20–21
erosion	6, 10–11
famines	12–13, 19
floods	16–21, 24
freshwater	6–7, 12, 15, 25–26
irrigation	24–25, 27
locks	22–23
peat bogs	29
plastic bottles	30–31
pollution	15, 30–31
population	6, 13, 17
rain	6, 9–11, 18–19, 24, 27
recycling	13, 26, 31
reservoirs	14, 20–21, 24–25
salt water	7, 13, 26
transportation	22, 31
Venice	5, 19
weathering	10–11
wetlands	7, 28–29